BREAKING THE POWER

OF UNKNOWN

COVENANT

Pastor Elijah Oluwole

Breaking The Power Of Unknown Covenant
Pastor Elijah
© 2014.

Published by
Beeni Global Resources
381, Borno Way,
Yaba,
Lagos, Nigeria.
PO Box 3405, Somolu,
Lagos, Nigeria.
Tel: +2348033225953/+2349096991619
beeniglobalresources@gmail.com

ISBN: 978-978-942-914-1

Other books in the True Deliverance Series:

Breaking The Power Of Unknown Spirit Husband and Spirit Wife.

Breaking The Power Of Unknown Curse.

Power Over Evil Handwriting.

Introduction

Wherefore hear the word of the Lord, ye scornful men that rule this people which is in Jerusalem; because you have said, we have made a covenant with death and with hell are we at agreement. When the overflowing scourge shall pass through, it shall not come unto us; for we have made lies our refuge and understand falsehood and have hid ourselves. Therefore thus says the Lord God, Behold, I lay in Zion for a foundation a stone, a tried, a precious stone, a sure foundation; he that believeth shall not make haste. Judgment also will lay to the line and righteousness to the plummet; and the hail shall sweep away the refuge of lies, and waters, and the waters shall overflow the hiding place. And your covenant with death shall be disannulled and your agreement with hell shall not stand: When the overflowing scourge shall pass through, then ye shall be trodden down by it. - Isaiah 28:14-18

Many people may not be able to grasp the full import of the title of this book because I have used the word 'covenant', like they would if I had titled it 'deliverance from generational bondage'.

A girl came here from one of the biggest churches in Nigeria and after praying for her and she saw what happened, she said "Pastor, I wish this truth could be preached in my church because we are in bondage in that church".

The 'Power of Unknown Covenant' is not the same as an 'Unknown Covenant'. The former is stronger and does not belong among common place knowledge. This book will prove invaluable in exposing this power that may have oppressed you the reader up until now.

The people who are suffering from delusion of some sorts will claim to be" under grace and not under a curse": how sad. Grace does not remove a curse, rather it teaches you the truth and the way of righteousness; and the more truth you know and obey, the more freedom you would have.

The Bible says in Titus 2:11-12

For the grace of God that brings salvation hath appeared to all men, teaching us that, denying ungodliness and worldly lusts, we should live soberly, righteously, and godly, in this present world;

It is clear from this passage that grace brings salvation and teaches one to live righteously, but does not break curses because curses and evil covenants do not come from God: they come from Satan through men.

By the time you are done reading, understanding and praying the prayers in this book seriously, you will obtain your freedom in Jesus name.

Covenant: Its Meaning

The Bible says in Mark 13:14

> "... let him who reads understand".

Until you understand who you are in Christ, you may not realize the volume of destruction that the power of unknown covenant has caused in many generations. This is why many Christians are limited and cannot confront the powers of darkness.

Covenants are cut with blood, and may not necessarily have to involve one's spirit at the initial stage. When you give your life to Christ, it is your spirit that becomes born again, neither your blood nor your soul. Your spirit becomes born again first, then your body. As for your soul, it becomes born again by continual meditation on the word of God. The more truth you know, the more your soul becomes born again and many more errors will be corrected.

The power of unknown covenant has hindered many Christians from entering into the blessing of the new covenant because the former was not voluntarily cut but was entered into by proxy.

A scripture in the book of Ezekiel comes to mind here,

which says:

"...*the soul that sinneth. It shall die.*" Ezekiel 18:20

That is to say that the sin of a father will not be visited on his son or daughter, every man shall bear own sin.

A sin is completely different from a covenant. If your father lived and died in sin, but you lived in sin and repented, your sins will be forgiven and you will become a child of God, but that will not remove the covenant your father cut on your behalf from your blood.

The reason for this clarification is this: many teachers of the word cannot separate these two, though they are totally different. It is taught by some pastors that once you are holy, sanctified, filled with the Holy Ghost, you are no more under the covenant of your father's house, you are free. But when you enter into a church in this generation, you will find out that three quarters of the members are suffering. They pay tithes, sow seeds, pray, fast for long days, and after all of these, there are no improvements.

We must know that there are rewards for obedience but one may not get the rewards for obedience if some covenants are still operational in his life; there is something that has been in existence through your bloodline before you were born.

If I may ask: Is your blood born again?

Born Again and Still In Bondage

If you have been in a church for twenty years, and you still sit down in the congregation, not a Pastor, nor a worker and you have been born again for twenty years, something in your blood is tying you down.

Many people have vigils and speak in tongues, but when they go to bed, a masquerade comes to attack them in the dream; definitely, something is still wrong somewhere.

If five of you line up for employment, and four candidates were shortlisted, but getting to your turn, you are given an excuse like: "we are very sorry, the chairman just left to attend an urgent meeting, you may have to come back next week", thus you are the only one that was rejected, something is wrong somewhere.

Or a man who promised to help you asked you to see him the next day, but when you eventually go to meet him, he avoids you by telling you he is not around, then brother (sister), something is wrong somewhere.

How can you be a graduate with good grades but cannot get a job that is commensurate to your certificate? Something is wrong somewhere.

I want to announce to you that the suffering, the hardship or whatever adversity you are going through is not from God. Poverty is not part of the agreement of being born again.

If you are of marriageable age, but keep referring to yourself as an eligible bachelor, claiming that you are special and still searching for the best, that problem will definitely make you marry a wrong person.

If you are a sister, ripe for marriage, yet no man has approached you to ask for your hand in marriage, you have a problem. You must know you are in serious bondage.

Yes you are born again, yes you attend church regularly, yes you are a worker in the church, filled with Holy Ghost and sanctified, exhibiting the fruit of the spirit, but when it get to matters of finance, you quickly get up and walk away because that is a no go area for you, giving excuses that Christianity does not allow wealth, that the little a righteous man has is better than the many riches of the ungodly, so the little you have is what you are managing, truth be told, poverty is in your bloodline. You need serious deliverance.

Why Many Christians Are Still In Bondage

I used to wonder why many Christians, who understand the bible and have faith in God, do not move forward in life. The reason for all these is the power of unknown covenant.

Let's look at Isaiah 28: 14-18

Wherefore hear the word of the Lord, ye scornful men that rule this people which is in Jerusalem; because you have said, we have made a covenant with death and with hell are we at agreement. When the overflowing scourge shall pass through, it shall not come unto us; for we have made lies our refuge and under falsehood and have hid ourselves. Therefore thus says the Lord God, Behold, I lay in Zion for a foundation a stone, a tried, a precious stone, a sure foundation; he that believeth shall not make haste. Judgment also will lay to the line and righteousness to the plummet; and the hail shall sweep away the refuge of lies, and waters, and the waters shall overflow the hiding place. And your covenant with death shall be disannulled and your agreement with hell shall not stand: When the overflowing scourge shall pass through, then ye shall be trodden down by it.

They have made a covenant with hell; it is not the people but the rulers of the people that made the covenant, and in the process have bound entire generations; that is why it is called 'generational covenant'.

Let us see what the bible says in the book of Exodus 20: 3-5 (although some Christians do not read that portion of the scripture under the guise of being a New Testament Christian, truth be told, many will gnash their teeth if they do not repent before it is too late, because God said If anybody takes away from my word, I will take his part out of the book of life - Revelation 22:19)

Thou shalt have no other god before me., thou shall not make unto thee any graven image or any likeness of anything that is in heaven above, or that is in the earth beneath or the water underneath the earth, thou shall not bow down thyself nor serve them for I the Lord, am a jealous God visiting the iniquities of the fathers upon the children unto the third and fourth generation of them that hate me and showing mercies on thousands of them that love me and keeping my commandments. Exodus 20: 3-6

God says when you go to serve an idol, you have committed the sin of idolatry, therefore He will visit His wrath on that generation from the 1st to the 4th

generation. Looking into the book of Isaiah 28:14 which was referred to earlier, it says the rulers of these people made a covenant with death, and an agreement with hell.

History tells us that our grandfathers and great grandfathers served idols and still serve them till date. They also made covenants with those idols, covenants that bind their unborn generations.

A covenant with an idol is a sin, but once you have repented from your sin and accepted Jesus Christ, the covenant is no more a sin; however, the covenant is still effective in your life because when the covenant was cut, some utterances were made concerning you and those utterances are powerful; those utterances are words and words live to perform what they are sent. The power behind the words of the covenant runs in your blood so you cannot run from the covenant. It matters not where you run to, you cannot escape it.

I decree over your life, any power of unknown covenant that troubles your life shall die, in Jesus name, Amen.

The covenant that was entered into on your behalf may be troubling your life, and until you break its power, reverse the words, or kill the power of the word that runs the covenant, you cannot enjoy the benefit of the covenant of our Lord Jesus Christ because the bible says He is

"... *the mediator of a new covenant... that speaketh better things than the blood of Abel".* Hebrews 12:24

The Covenant in the blood of Jesus speaks greater things. There are lots of benefits in this covenant that you ought to enjoy like life, blessings, breakthroughs, unlimited open doors that the enemy cannot reverse.

True Life Testimonies

A young couple who are both evangelists minister to lots of people and through them, God sets those people free; but, they beg to eat. The wife holds a B.sc degree and whenever she attended a job interview, she was never taken, until someone told her about our ministry and she came for prayers.

While prayers were ongoing for her, something strange happened: a personality came up, and the generational spirit in her opened up and spoke. The spirit said although she is a child of God, (it's obvious they know if you are a child of God) and she has accepted that righteous man (Jesus), but her ancestors made a covenant with him that when she grows up, she would serve him and when she serves him, he would bless her because all her blessings and greatness were exchanged through the covenant.

I asked the spirit what she should do and it said, she would only need to take a little step: she will buy red oil, go to where he is in her village and pour it on his head; then he will release all her blessings in his possession and keep blessing her.

Then I told the demon that there is no problem, but we will worship him in a new manner. It asked me to repeat what I said and I did. I said," sister, the spirit wants oil on its head, now begin to pour the oil of the blood of Jesus". That was how the covenant was broken and I till today, the sister's blessing has not stopped flowing: somebody bought her a car and now, she travels all around the world.

Another experience:

A sister, a child of God and a minister of the gospel, never knew that she had a covenant over her head until she got married and started having children. Her first child died and people consoled her, telling her to trust in the Lord. There are many words of consolation and encouragement from people telling you to trust in the Lord that will do you no good.

How would your child die and you will be able to rejoice?

This sister did not bother to ask God why her first child died and she went on to have the second one that died also. This time, they gathered prayer warriors and prayed that God would give her another child because all they believed in is holiness; they also believe that once you are saved, you are saved and there is nothing like breaking of covenants.

God gave her another child, but on the day of the baby's naming ceremony, she was in the process of bathing the child when she left the child in the basin to go check what she had on the heat. Before she came back, the child had died.

At this moment the church knew there was a problem but they did not know how to fix it, so they kept on praying until one brother rose up and suggested a visit to the sister. The brother in question is a violent prayer warrior hence on their arrival at the sister's home; he asked her if there was a covenant over her head. She got annoyed and told the brother she was not comfortable with his question; she asked him whether he was calling her a witch. When people have been members of a church for so long, there is every possibility that they rise to certain positions. You may be made a Minister, Pastor, Choir leader or Head of department, and because of that think you don't or wouldn't have any problem or attacks: that was exactly what the sister was passing through.

At this juncture, the prayer warrior and his team explained to her that they asked her that question because they wanted to get to the root of the problem, but she told them that if they wanted to pray, they could go ahead and pray.

The brother led the prayer. As soon as he started to pray, the voice of the sister turned to that of a man and something shouted from within her:

"Were you there when the mother came to ask for her from us? Were you there when the mother made a covenant with us? Were you there when the mother gave her to me as a wife? Pastor the covenant is real."

The sister's husband sat by the side witnessing the whole deliverance process (this is why we sometimes record the video of deliverance sessions so the victim can see how the demon(s) were speaking through him or her.

After much prayer, the covenant was broken. This sister I'm talking about is now an evangelist and a minister with a lot of miracles happening through her. A hidden covenant had been holding her bound; that is why we call it power of the unknown covenant.

I do not know the covenant that is following you, your husband or your wife, but I know the power of God, through prayers, will break and nullify it in Jesus name.

A covenant is no respecter of persons. If you believe that a covenant affects only church members without going near the head, you are deceiving yourself.

This one will shock you. In a particular church, messages on deliverance are never preached, just like in many churches today. There was a Pastor in the church who had no child. The General Overseer and the entire church prayed for him to no avail. The pastor's predicament shocked the General Overseer because the Pastor was such a wonderful man.

Finally, the Pastor's wife got pregnant and the whole church became agog with rejoicing.

Sometimes God may delay one's miracle because when the breakthrough takes place while the beneficiary is still bound by some unknown covenant, the breakthrough can kill him.

The Pastor's wife gave birth to a baby boy, and on the day the baby was born, the Pastor died. As soon as news reached him, the General Overseer started praying, asking God to do some miracle by raising the dead Pastor, but God said He couldn't wake up, he is gone forever. They asked God why (a question they should have asked a long time ago), and God told them to go his father's house where his people were still mourning him.

The Overseer went to the Pastor's hometown. He was sitting down when an old woman came out and said, "We thought it is finished. They said he was born again, that he was a fire -spitting Pastor; when will this end, when shall be the end of all these evil?"

The old woman continued, "When the grandfather was born, the great grandfather died, and when his own father was born, the grandfather died, when he himself was born, his father died now his son has been born, he has died, when will it stop?".

The General Overseer said he did not know when tears gushed out from his eyes, and said to himself "so truly there is a generational bondage".

Words of evil covenant may follow you for life and you will not know that the word is following your life, but many problems will manifest to prove that there is a problem.

Some people have witchcraft spirit but they do not know.

There was a Pastor's wife who had been barren for a long time. I prayed for her and when I told her she has a familiar spirit in her life she quickly said "God forbid"; she jumped up , looked at me and went wild. Since I was not the one who had problems, I concluded she was not interested in being delivered so to be sure, I asked her if she wanted to go and she said "yes".

 She ran to the person that introduced her to me and said, "That small Pastor called me a witch. If the senior Pastor did not call me that, why should the small Pastor call me such a name? I will report him to the Senior Pastor" and the man responded," look if Pastor Elijah said you have a familiar spirit, just go and ask him the way out".

It was her great grandmother that bequeathed marine spirit to her. When the old woman was about to die, her co- witches asked her who her replacement would be and she looked into the future and dedicated the lady.

The grandma died many years before she was born. When that covenant was broken, two months later she got pregnant.

Conclusion

I know many teachers of the word today are twisting things due to their ulterior motives, but my friend you should not miss it: you need to break that covenant. I do not know the one that is following you but I am very sure that through the power of prayers I have broken the one that followed my life.

For some people, their own problems are unknown curses, and others are battling evil hand writing.

All you need to do is pray and break this covenant. Break it over your son, break it over your daughter, and break it over your generation. It is a very serious prayer God will show you mercy and it will be broken.

I have seen people who are wizards but do not know they are wizards, I have seen people who have serious marine spirit but do not know they have it though they speak in tongues. Look at their faces very well when they are speaking in tongues and you will see the Queen of the coast sitting inside them cool and untouched, shinning like gold, by the time they pray for you and say be free in Jesus name and you get home, you find yourself eating in the dream but today as you are reading this book the covenant shall be broken in Jesus name.

All you need to do is:

(1) Repent from your sin.

(2) Surrender your life to Jesus and become a child of God. To do this, pray as follows:

> Lord, I am a sinner, please forgive all my sins. Jesus come into my life and be my personal Lord and Saviour, in Jesus' name I pray.

Now that you are a child of God, pray the covenant breaking prayers in this book and the power of God shall break the covenant in Jesus' name.

Prayer Points

In the name of Jesus, every satanic pollution in my life, blood of Jesus, wipe them away.

In the name of Jesus, unknown covenant upon my head, that turned me into a nobody, your time is up, break in Jesus' name.

In the name of Jesus, unknown covenant on my head, unknown covenant on my children's heads, unknown covenant on my wife's head, unknown covenant on my grandchildren's heads, what are you waiting for, break.

In the name of Jesus, the power that is supervising the unknown covenant on my head, your time is up, die

In the name of Jesus, O God arise and break every chain of evil covenant over my life.

Arrow of evil covenant in my life, hear the word of the Lord, die.

In the name of Jesus, powers controlling unknown covenant in my life, appear;

Now that you have appeared, from today I am no longer under your control, my husband is no longer under your control, my children are no longer under your control, and my grandchildren are no longer under your control in Jesus name.

Anything that my grandfather has been giving you that you are now demanding from me, I give to you by the blood of Jesus, receive it now!

All my breakthroughs in your hand, by the judgment of fire, release them and die in Jesus name.

In the name of Jesus, I recover all my breakthroughs now and forever.

www.ingramcontent.com/pod-product-compliance
Lightning Source LLC
Chambersburg PA
CBHW060550030426
42337CB00021B/4523